Walkin' In Bergen
A Kid's Guide To Bergen, Norway

Photography by John D. Weigand
Poetry by Penelope Dyan

Bellissima Publishing, LLC
Jamul, California
www.bellissimapublishing.com

Copyright © 2017 by Penny D. Weigand and John D. Weigand

All rights reserved. No part of this book may be
reproduced or transmitted in any form or by any means,
electronic or mechanical, including photocopying,
recording, or by any other means, or by any information or
storage retrieval system, without permission from the publisher.

ISBN 978-1-61477-271-2
First Edition

"Walking through life is one big adventure!"

Penelope Dyan

Walkin' In Bergen
Bellissima Publishing, LLC

Introduction

Bergen sits on the west coast of Norway. Trading began in the 1020's. Founded in 1070 by King Olav Kyrre, four years after the Viking Age ended with the Battle of Hastings, the city was called jørgvin, which means "the green meadow among the mountains." It was the capital of Norway throughout the 13th century. The German Kontor, established in 1360, remained for 400 years, monopolizing trade in fish and fish oil. Bergen had exclusive rights to mediate all trade between Northern Norway and abroad until 1789 and it was also the largest city in Norway until the 1830s, when Oslo became the capital of Norway, and was Norway's largest city. What remains of the quays, Bryggen, is a World Heritage Site. Hit by many fires over the years, Bergen kept on rebuilding itself and is a monument to the perseverance of its people. Today's houses date back to 1702.

Get ready to see some fun things, as you turn the pages of this early reader, created by award winning author, attorney and former teacher, Penelope Dyan, and photographer, John D. Weigand. Then look for the free music video that goes with this book (on the Bellissimavideo YouTube channel) and see even more of this beautiful place!

Walkin' In Bergen
Bellissima Publishing, LLC

Walkin' In Bergen
A Kid's Guide To Bergen, Norway

Photography by John D. Weigand
Poetry by Penelope Dyan

When you go walking
through Bergen, Norway,
you just might find a moose or two!
But since they will
most likely be toy moose,
you'll know JUST what to do!
You can take that moose
right off that store shelf,
and buy that toy moose
for your very OWN self!

The oldest part of Bergen
is still around,
although several times
it has burned
right to the ground.
The people keep rebuilding things
right where they've always stood,
tall and straight of sturdy wood.

You see, the people here
really do care,
as they carefully build and rebuild
EACH handrail AND stair. . .
all so that YOU don't have to stop,
as you climb those stairs
right up to the top!

This German built area
where German traders once
traded their wares,
is oh so VERY colorful that
EVERYONE just stares!

And THIS ship at port
tells its very OWN tale,
about ALL the ships
that came from here,
and once took sail!

Bergen was once called Jarvin
(which means the green meadow
beneath the mountains.)
So up into the mountains you go,
not TOO fast and NOT too slow!
And mom doesn't mind one single bit,
because instead of walking,
MOM gets to SIT!

Below THIS mountain
is a beautiful scene
of houses, blue water and boats
AND grass of green!

Finally, up on the mountain top, you find a GREAT place to play! And you ask your mom politely, "Can we PLEASE stay ALL day?"

Mom says,
"We can stay for awhile if you wish,"
as you wait for YOUR turn to
swing in a dish!

You see a climbing, sliding toy, perfect for a girl or boy!

Then, after you have played awhile,
you see a troll with a friendly smile!
After bidding the troll a sad, "Adieu,"
Mom says,
"It's back to the hotel for us and you!"
Cheerfully, you go on your way,
because you have had a perfect day!

And as as through Bergen,
and back to the hotel you wend,
Dad sighs and says,
"Every good thing
must come to an end."
And then you don't feel quite so bad,
because (after all)
you have a GREAT Mom and Dad!
And tomorrow with the break of day,
you will hop on that train
and you will be on your way.

"Twenty years from now you will be more disappointed by the things that you didn't do than by the ones you did do. So throw off the bowlines. Sail away from the safe harbor. Catch the trade winds in your sails. Explore. Dream. Discover."

MARK TWAIN

www.ingramcontent.com/pod-product-compliance
Ingram Content Group UK Ltd.
Pitfield, Milton Keynes, MK11 3LW, UK
UKHW060135240426
12048UKWH00002B/50